Cider Press Review

PO Box 33384, San Diego, CA 92163
Marketing: 619.269.9469 | ciderpressreview.com

Cider Press is pleased to send you this book for review:

The Acrobatic Company of the Invisible
Poems

George Looney

84 pages, 6 x 9
ISBN: 9781930781634
$18.95 PAPER

Publication Date: August 1, 2023

Please send 2 copies or PDF of any published review.

Contact: Caron Andregg / Catherine Friesen
619.269.9469 | info@ciderpressreview.com

The Acrobatic Company
of the Invisible

THE ACROBATIC COMPANY OF THE INVISIBLE

POEMS BY GEORGE LOONEY

Cider Press Review
San Diego

Cider Press Review
PO BOX 33384
San Diego, CA, USA
ciderpressreview.com

First edition
10 9 8 7 6 5 4 3 2 1 0

ISBN: 9781930781634
Library of Congress Control Number: 2023938590
Cover image: *Goldfinch* from *In Flight*, © Mark Harvey, courtesy
    Mark Harvey Photography, LTD, MARK-HARVEY.COM
Author photograph by Robert Frank
Book design by Caron Andregg

Winner of the 2022 *Cider Press Review* Editors' Prize Book Award:
CIDERPRESSREVIEW.COM/BOOKAWARD.

Printed in the United States of America
at Bookmobile in Minneapolis, MN USA.

in memory of my parents and my brother

Also by George Looney

Poetry

Birds of Sympathy: Correspondences (with Douglas Smith) (2023)
Ode to the Earth in Translation (2021)
The Itinerate Circus: New and Selected Poems 1995-2020 (2020)
What Light Becomes: The Turner Variations (2019)
Hermits in Our Own Flesh: The Epistles of an Anonymous Monk (2016)
Meditations Before the Windows Fail (2015)
Structures the Wind Sings Through (2014)
Monks Beginning to Waltz (2012)
A Short Bestiary of Love and Madness (2011)
Open Between Us (2010)
The Precarious Rhetoric of Angels (2005)
Greatest Hits 1990-2000 (2001)
Attendant Ghosts (2000)
Animals Housed in the Pleasure of Flesh (1995)

Fiction

The Visibility of Things Long Submerged (2023)
The Worst May Be Over (2020)
Report from a Place of Burning (2018)
Hymn of Ash (2008)

Acknowledgements

Some of the poems in this collection first appeared in the magazines cited, often in earlier versions:

Albatross: "Palimpsest Vespers" and "Early Light in Erie"
Ambit (England): "Tattoo of a Road Runner"
Book of Matches: "Despite Heraclitus"
Cimarron Review: "The Romans Made Gods of Their Ancestors"
Cloudbank: "The Hip Bones of a Woman as Runes"
Concho River Review: "Studio Musician with Trembling Hands and
    Maker's on His Breath"
Crab Orchard Review: "Psalms on Sheet Metal with Margaritas"
Dispatches (online): "Hummingbird and Window," "To Die in Erie,
    Pennsylvania," and "Before All Hell Breaks Loose"
Flying South: "Wayward Guardian Angels" and "Rituals in Lingerie and
    Insomnia"
The Gettysburg Review: "After the Carnival Closes Down"
Ilanot Review: "Make It New, He Said"
The Laurel Review: "The Lyrical Prophesies of a Spanish Guitar" and "The
    Girl Who Made Love in Cemeteries"
Louisiana Literature: "What Stone's on Hand"
The Missouri Review: "The Consolation of a Company of Acrobats,"
    "A Temporary Delaying of the Inevitable," "Early Pastoral," and "To
    Account for Such Grace"
Nimrod International Journal: "On the Eaves of the House Next Door"
Paterson Literary Review: "Last Words to My Father"
Prairie Schooner: "Swear Not by the Moon, th' Inconstant Moon"
Prism Review: "A Glissando on the Quietest Instrument," "The Carcass of
    What Was," and "Almost a Sonnet on a Train to Points West"
Raritan: "A Study in the Opacity of Memory and Lingerie," "Leaving a
    Place of Smoke and Dire Prophesies," and "Stories of Blue Herons in
    Winter"
RCC MUSE Literary Journal: "The Singing of Accidental Larks"
Slant: "With Walt Whitman in a Couple of Hotel Rooms"

Willows Wept Review: "The Music Sparrows Add"
Voices Israel: "The Bestowing of Grace in Perry Square" and "Soundtrack for Mystery in a Field of Muddy Angels"

The four poems published in *The Missouri Review* won the 2010 Jeffrey E. Smith Editors' Prize in Poetry.

"The Music Sparrows Add" was a semifinalist for *December's* 2022 Jeff Marks Memorial Poetry Prize.

Contents

These may be
the dead, the sick, those gone into rage

and madness, gone bad, but they're our dead
and our sick, and we will slake their lips
with our very hearts if we must, and we must.

—William Matthews

The Bestowing of Grace in Perry Square

This could be the origin of pointillism,
this gazebo fractured by what light can do

left to its own devices. Even grackles
hop different in this light, stippled,

the misbegotten purple sheen of
their mercurial necks slipping from dull

to brilliant again and again. Everything
bejeweled this morning, as if remembered.

After all, memory bestows grace
the way this speckling of light

baptizes the gazebo and the grass
and the birds in the grass into a living psalm,

praise what everything was always about.

A Glissando on the Quietest Instrument

The mystical curve and angle of the bare shoulder
of a woman asleep at four in the morning.

The light that gives this pale amalgam of flesh
and bone its allure comes from outside,

from what remains of a moon through where the curtains
don't touch. The nearby, dimmer glow from

the streetlamp hums what could be mistaken for
a lullaby in a foreign tongue. You'd swear it is

her shoulders themselves that are glowing, and this
isn't a lullaby but a classic blues riff. Loss, you'd say,

is a single malt elixir that goes down so smooth
what it leaves in passing isn't so much a throat

as a glissando played on the quietest instrument
imaginable. Maybe this woman's bare shoulder

illumined by a four-in-the-morning moon could be
the perfect answer for any sorrow you'd sing.

Palimpsest Vespers

Wrens wring dirges out of a sky where nothing musical
lasts for long, their innumerable bodies brittle notes,

embellishment for some sorrow we cannot bear. Such
lift and flurry of feathers and grace is almost enough

to convince someone heading home in this
bird-infested dusk to start to dance. Say it's a woman.

Say a lover she left years ago has died and she is
remembering a night when, naked and damp in bed,

they listened to the blessed varieties of evening birdsong,
those winged vespers with furious hearts, and tried

to mimic each in turn between bouts of laughter
and kisses. Say nothing for her since has matched

the music they made as his fingers slipped inside her
and his mouth found hers again and the bird cries

continued out in the evening as if in accompaniment.
Say the past is nothing if not a soundtrack for loss.

The Lyrical Prophesies of a Spanish Guitar

Late November. The bare limbs of trees
      want to deny
the scuttled urgency of clouds

that scurry and seem to compose ballads
      an old man plays,
remembering the nearly forgotten

scents of a woman who would sing damp
      beside him in bed,
the strumming of an out-of-tune Spanish guitar

a sad backdrop after love. Nothing
      can explain the harsh
unforgiving style of this fog, how,

despite it being no more than a dampness
      in what is only
the cool of an autumn morning,

it's as impatient as something more
      solid, say this
woman in earth-tones with a son in tow

who can't be more than seven, his frantic
      hand collapsed inside
hers, larger and more insistent. It's almost

as if her hand's a Spanish ballad and his
          the repeated phrase,
a delicate, familial theme. Missing

in his are the variations, which always
          and only come
with time. Or is that come *as* time?

The morning fog takes on the images of
          their passing through it
so that, for a frenzied instant, their being

in a rush hangs in a series of interlocked
          and vague tropes
of her body that are shivered through

again and again by the irregular form
          of the reluctant boy
enslaved to this headlong scurry of flesh

and fallen cloud. There's music in this fog,
          though it's not
the lyrical prophesies of a Spanish guitar

in tune and strummed by a lover who knows
          the sturdy instrument
like the inflections of his own body

but the hollow sounds of some weathered wind
          instrument, a music
made by someone's shopworn breath forced

into the confines of a columned space and released
        in fingered patterns.
The music you'd hear standing in front of

Hopper's *Hotel by a Railroad.* Outside
        it might be
starting to snow. Here there's only

the indignation of late afternoon
        light filtered by
residue that leaves a dour patina

on the sills of windows that can't
        be opened.
The forgetfulness of how the woman

in the slip curls into the inevitability
        of her body
imbues the austere room with a scent,

maybe one the man wants to recall
        through the stink
and nervous ruin of his cigarette.

Any music left between them—these
        figures of lamentation
posed in this regret of a rented room,

one looking down at the pages
        of a book she has
read enough to turn the words

into notes she hums lackadaisically
   and the other
looking out at tracks that could be

staves for a music that could get fog
   up and dancing—
must be an almost jaunty dirge

all about time and how to remember
   any detail ends up
elevating loss to the level of the sacred.

Which is what the Spanish guitar,
   played by a lover
to the beloved while, outside,

everything's offered a kind of redemption
   by the laying on
of a discordant fog, claims for us all,

even if the guitar's out of tune
   and played poorly,
a music to forgive everyone who listens.

The Music Sparrows Add

for Mark Doty

The oldest arrogance is to think
knowing makes anything
better. To let the dead
have a say

in what music the leaves dance
an elegant tarantella to
with sparrows on the edge
of the rain-soaked feeder

is to give in
to cliché. It was dark
when the rain started, the moon
new, no light

coming through the clouds, or from under,
power out for blocks.
Nothing to spark drops
into anything else. This can't be

all there is. To whistle
the tune rain and leaves conspired
to fill the dark with
now, in this light

filled with the subtle
flitting hues of sparrows,

is to remember
and celebrate. To dance,

following the lead of leaves,
is one way to forgive
all arrogance. Don't
think. Remember

the music sparrows add
to the verdant fervor
of these fragrant and wind-jostled
leaves. Experience

is the sound within
every body. To hear it,
listen with the faith
that lets sparrows leap into air.

A Study in the Opacity of Memory and Lingerie

The moon, this morning, is a lesson
in the peripheral,
fraying a way to speak

of what happens. Loss doesn't
need much light,
and we all remember

we started as soil. As kids,
our mothers yelling *How is it*
you can get so filthy

sitting there in your suit?
before church taught us the truth
of this. And circuses

travelled between towns
with names like The Unfathomable
Perfidy of Amazement

and set up in fallow fields,
tamping down the dirt
with the stoic heft of elephants

to form the center ring, where
the moon itself
would be brought down

for the delight of the crowd only
to be dismantled,
packed away and carted off

to the next town after
the grand finale. A woman
has always been enough

to convince me no trick is
worth it without
the hint it might be

magic. When that lovely glitter
of the assistant steps
in the box that will make her

disappear, the music, no matter
how corny, how
canned it is, assumes

the grace of Mozart playing for
all he's worth
for his father's ghost. If there

is dust in the air, dances
vaguely European
and without a doubt stately

in the best sense form themselves
to the music. It is
all misdirection, I've heard it

said. No such thing as magic.
Hearing *It's a study*
in the peripheral is all

it takes to remind me how
the moon was
diaphanous, a negligee

thrown off for the sake of
the magic innate
in every naked body

we keep with us, memory
a little frayed
at the edges, but still

happening.

Of the Body Proper

No absence is
a remedy
for the lack of touch.

Reason says to
ignore this
woman's shoulders, runes

that insist on being
chanted, a rough
translation of sunlight

into a tongue no one has
spoken long enough
to hear it

as a longing of the body
proper. Syntax
can't clarify

the sanctity of
any object's intent.
To explain desire

as emptiness filling
the body isn't
as incongruous

as the thought of a crow
etching, from
a hollowed-out sky,

the one sentence
able to contain
longing. These shoulders

curve light into elaborate
librettos in which
longing's an aria manifesting

what not even time is
formless
enough to contain.

Psalms on Sheet Metal with Margaritas

Early morning October rain on the tin roof
of a mobile home's added-on porch
is what the dead hear the first few years
they are dead, listening from rocking chairs,
sipping margaritas, and remembering
whatever they have to remember so they can
smile, remembering. The dead who've been
dead long enough not even the taste of raw

oysters could lure them into thinking they are
alive and smoking stogies under a tin roof
on which a steady rain intones psalms,
they know history never gets it right, that regret
is a parasite that doesn't die with the flesh.
Some not-long dead are out walking in a cold rain
the living don't know. When a couple hears music
coming from the cracked-open window of a car

trolling by, they do their best to take each other
in their lost arms and dance, while those
dead longer play cards and smoke under the tin roof
rain is trying to turn elemental and dissolve.
The dead ignore the living every bit as much
as the living ignore the dead. Which means
now and then one of the dead is surprised
by a woman stepping out of a shower, how

water glistens on her like some foreign language
inscribed on her skin. A holy text, no doubt,

a dead man says out loud, to no one. Though
maybe the shivering woman's thinking of
a former lover a friend's told her has died,
and as she pulls a towel around herself
says to no one *Who's there?* Say the dead
tallying up points for bridge on the porch

sip their margaritas and turn toward the woman
and the water that, clinging to her body
and catching what light there is, could be trying to
say something that would make everything,
finally, make sense. Say no palimpsest
of water over skin could record anything
the dead and the living could agree on. Say
the dead man thinks the towel-draped woman

can hear him and, thinking this, starts talking
to her about what it's like to be dead
and to know it. The dead trying to bluff
each other under the tin roof being rained on
shake their heads, knowing any second
the dead man who's talking will stop, understanding
the absurdity of trying to stretch out
the interstices when being straddles non-being

like a lover, and the ragged hermit of his heart
will whisper to him that memory's not to be
trusted. October's music—half-sister
to a drummer's brush on a hi-hat cymbal,
rain on a tin roof—is all about remembering.
Not even the viscous memory of oysters
sliding down a throat with a hint of lime
and the benediction of salt is enough

to build a solid bridge over the briny waters
that lie between the living and the dead.
Let those who can dance in the rain dance.
Let the rain finish whatever message it has to
finish in crude Morse code on the tin roof.
Let both the living and the dead let go of
the burden of that message and whisper
to lovers who hear the whispers and smile.

The Girl Who Made Love in Cemeteries

It's the thought of them down there looking up,
she said. The shifting shape of our bodies
coming between them and constellations
they've whispered the stories of for so long
it seems they have no room for anything
more. That's what does it for me, giving them
something new to whisper under the earth.
Whether flat on my back on a marble
headstone, or standing, with you behind, me
hugging this stone angel for all she's worth.

The Consolation of a Company of Acrobats

These children in my father's house. He asks
his wife, a woman who is more in this world,

Why are they here? What is it they want?
he asks her, not ready, it seems, to speak to them,

to give in completely to them being there. In
the old days, we might have called them harbingers.

Now the word's *dementia.* We say nothing's there,
though we rarely say it to him. Humor him,

a friend of the family says. But there's no humor
here, only a future bleak and brief. I want

to see these children my father sees and do what he can't,
to ask them what it is they mean. The gall of it,

life. To rob us of all we think of as who we are
and offer, as if in compensation, cherubic children

who point at us but are invisible. At his best,
he knows they don't belong in his house, and says so.

Other times, he chuckles at the tricks they do
as if they're there to entertain him. Distraction

is an art even the most healthy mind practices.
To call up children not there, children who are

whimsical and who smile at him as they somersault
off the couch, is this compensation for the failure

of his eyes? These comic acrobats he can see
even if the rooms they frolic in get darker every day,

they're not angels, as his wife tells me she likes to believe
they are. Could they be some skewed sliver

of memory, maybe from earlier than memory
is supposed to form? Are the darkening rooms

he stumbles through, leaning on his cane, the womb,
these children his brothers and sisters never born?

Do they come to make him comfortable with what waits
after his body finally gives out, the place where having

been born and lived and died can't be distinguished
from never having been born? If so, maybe his wife

has it right. Maybe they *are* angels, and there's no heaven
better than the acrobatic company of the invisible.

Wayward Guardian Angels

They like to fuck with the technical
gadgets of TV's Ghost Hunters,

whispering nonsense the men believe
to be the dead trying to tell them

something, to score big in sweeps week.
Black and white film noirs from the forties

and fifties keep them up late, seeing
themselves lurching from shadowed alleys

to the haggard niches of doorways
where desperate lovers have whispered

sentences in one another's ears
the rest of us know only get said in films

where everything's scripted. Spontaneity
can't be said to breathe in black and white,

especially when an organ's playing
desperate hymns in the distance too flat

to be authentic, and the woman's lips seem
red even in black and white, more real

than anything she says. Saints, it turns out,
can't bluff. Angels take them to the cleaners

in poker. Their winnings get them time off
so they can hang out with the living

where they watch repeats of the old films
they know by heart. They love how

we let ourselves forget the imagination
is a kind of memory. The angels aren't

looking out for the living. They are
watching over the dead, who can't do anything

for themselves anymore. Until the day
the dead are called out of the earth

by a single note blasted on a horn
by an archangel's breath, the angels are

responsible for the dreams the dead dream.
The angels are partial to ghost stories,

and both the recent dead and the long dead
find it easy to get into tales of haunting.

Some remember late night television
from before cable, before satellite TV.

All those Vincent Price films, or Lon
Chaney, father and son. Ghost stories help

the dead feel at home in the earth.
It's the living the angels like to fuck with,

pretending to be the dead and whispering,
just barely audible, a name or a phrase,

broken and mangled a bit, just enough
to keep it from being any sort of proof.

Time Was...

No one ever said it would be easy, this groping
after something as unforgiving as meaning.

Time was things were more definite, less prone to being
mistaken. Time was, old folks say. What follows has

a habit of stinking of hyperbole and a rough dismissal
of the present as having anything to do with grace.

Not to mention there's no music to it, this
atonal and unfortunate moment we live in. A time

when rivers cringe with shame. Leastways that's
what it smells like, an old timer says from his bench

atop what used to be, back in the day, a lock. Now
it's an open-air museum, a recovered fragment of concrete

and memory that no longer functions but still is,
the old timer says, a might prettier than that

dang factory they put up across the way, his
shaky attempt to point confusing the gulls

dipping low over us thinking, no doubt, of bread
cast into the sky. Gestures can be so imprecise.

Time was, words were enough to live by.

Soundtrack for Mystery
in a Field of Muddy Angels

Cows low miraculous psalms under a callous moon
that's all the light I have in which to see

the arches of the faces this music rises out of,
brutish and yet as graceful as any articulation

in paint or plaster of angels. I'm writing to
a distant woman. Behind me, inside the house,

my wife and her parents are practicing music,
a concerto for violin and piano Mozart put down

in a drunken fervor long enough ago
the alcohol is gone and all that remains

is the fervor. Mozart must have felt the sort
of ache the woman I write to is. The devout

lowing of cows in the field across the road
seems a proper accompaniment to the raw rendition

of Mozart starting up inside the lit-up house
I will have to go back in to soon. What each of us

carries inside us is too awful to be articulated
by something as divine as even the most inept music.

Studio Musician with Trembling Hands
and Maker's on His Breath

If my guitar sees fit to misalign
as many hearts as might hear it, it's not
my fault. Heck, the bugger in my own chest
ain't immune, despite the skull and cross bones
tattooed on its hardened left ventricle.
Though it's hard up for smokes and without hope
of parole, a sad tune played by fingers
bruised and experienced in the despair
of absence can have it down on its knees
and broken, like any fossil, by loss.

The Romans Made Gods of Their Ancestors

We all have them in our houses, often
on our walls—the dead we keep with us, still
and outside time, edged in light that's not
natural, posed by the lack of motion. This

one was taken in front of a window at night
in an airport—a son, his arms around his parents,
departure tingeing each memorial of a face.
The only one visible still living, the son is

so different, now, he can barely recognize himself
then. Light has no ethics, he knows, no need
for any accuracy it can't achieve. Regret isn't
in the light or in the grave. Absence is

something no photograph can be said to capture.
That flash reflected in the dark window
is nothing but the intersection of space and time
and four bodies in motion toward different departures.

Hummingbird and Window

Relativism isn't just theory
when this hummingbird shivers with itself
in a street-level storefront window

while a late morning sun rants
in the nine stories of glare that don't have
a hummingbird to disrupt

the argument light's having with everything
visible. To select anything so
slight, so shimmering, to notice

is to deny any theory
which would ignore the subtle
hum of the near-to-invisible.

Tattoo of a Road Runner

To paint a wall as white and unfulfilled
as a stray thought and still have someone

declare it beautiful, that's one hell
of a trick. To hear someone down

in the street at three in the morning
shouting *Story's not enough* is enough

to make you wonder how drunk you'd have to be
to say such a thing, quietly, to a friend,

much less to shout it on a street lit
only by the handful of streetlights visible

from a hotel window and a disgruntled moon.
For no reason you can come up with,

what comes to you is the road runner
you followed through a parking lot wavering

in the afternoon heat of Tucson, Arizona.
How its startling body made you want

to take chaos out for dinner and drinks
and later roll it for whatever it had

on it and leave it to sober up in a wash.
How that almost unnatural bird flew up

to perch on a fence before it dropped
to the other side and was gone

is what you remember. How that bird
you had heard couldn't fly, that was famous

for running—named, in fact, for it—flew,
that's what you can't get over, what startles

you still. Though there's no story to it
and no reason for that itinerant road runner

to come to you in a spartan hotel room
at three in the morning in a city named for

one of the great lakes with a drunk outside
who has stopped shouting and is crying,

relieving himself behind the hotel's dumpsters.
No reason you should believe he's crying

for a woman whose face he can't get
quite right, remembering it. A woman

he made laugh while they painted the walls
of a house they meant to live in. Who,

after he told her the story of the startling
road runner one night as they rested

on damp sheets after love, had a road runner
tattooed between her shoulder blades. To lose

such a woman would be reason enough,
you think, to cry and to shout things

you couldn't defend into a night sky
that ignored you. Such loss deserves to have

been painted by Hopper, the desert light
coming in through some stark hotel window

turning the transient body of a woman
in a beige slip into a bright landscape

where a long-legged bird runs toward the vague
shape of a man off in the distance,

far enough off to waver in the heat.
How Hopper manages to create

the illusion, in paint, of the wavering
is the best trick of all, and startling.

Rituals in Lingerie and Insomnia

Dressed in the lingerie of the emphatic, the moon
entices this storm to let everything go. South
of here, a woman slips into a black camisole and grins

at the idea of any man trying to ignore his nature
getting drunk in a tavern where the dust of the exotic
is nightly wiped off the bar. It's been said nothing is

more elegant than the curve, in the right light,
of a woman's hip bones. In the black camisole,
the woman could well be mocking the moon

and its desperate and feeble attempts at luridness,
or she could be paying homage. So often
nothing more than intent separates what we love

and what we tolerate. The saying is, the woman
has a compromising photo of the moon.
If you're willing to pay what she asks, you can

see it. When she slips the blurred photo out of
the waist of her jeans, past the hieroglyph for
passion the curve of her hip bone's become, you

don't have a chance. You'd pay anything for
just a glimpse. It's the moon, after all,
and many have been maddened by the longing

for her luminescent body. She has often been
blamed for everyone being out of sorts
the nights that, full of wine, she staggers through

what's left of the sky. Not even the longing
to hold the moon and keep her safe in your arms
till she sobers up excuses the gentrification of

the night sky. There's often almost nothing
between devastation and the quiet, inner lives
of men and women who only want what they've been told

to want. Longing is, in the end, every bit
as fickle as you suspected. The pornographic
moon pics were photo-shopped, and nothing you have

believed in remains free of suspicion. Off
in another country, a frail *matador de toros* shrouds
the bones, reconstructed with precision, of a bull

with his *capote.* Dust taunts the indifferent ghosts
in the stands. The moon, in a fluid Spanish,
croons a love ballad drenched in *duende*

and reminiscent of a lurid fable the woman
in the black camisole whispered in your ear
one night after sex, so explicit and so the opposite

of intimate that you cringed. You didn't want to
see the pictures she said she had, and you couldn't
imagine touching such an exquisite woman,

though her elegant clavicle and neck and chest
had gone red as a result of you having touched her.
Such rendezvous can be a side-effect of not enough

sleep, it's been said. Mundane hallucinations become
so real the waking world—where the moon is
naked and without language in the distance that is

the night sky—isn't discernible from the world
in which your three-in-the-morning house is haunted
by an ex-lover, a dead brother, and a cat whose ashes

rest in a clay vessel on the mantle. When ghosts
and visions get together, desire staggers, drunk
and muttering to itself, into the kitchen for coffee

steaming and black enough a woman could wear it
for lingerie and not be anything but irresistible—
maddening, actually. Longing haunts us more

than the dead do, more than a storm that wants to
turn us from the moon and all the lavish promises
it makes in Spanish or some long-dead language.

Make It New, He Said

A dried sprig of sage, not far from dust,
tucked into a book not read since

a woman's mouth was a Chinese character
no ink could etch out of a sky

so blank and unpronounceable the past
held no sway and had to scramble for

any vestige of significance. Memory is
all about what's gone, or gone missing.

Pound wanted poetry to bring the past
into the present, but nothing lost can be

written any clearer in the Latin alphabet
than in the eastern cages of precise ink strokes

he never got right. If the past is anything,
a desiccate sprig of sage can illuminate

the first letter of the one language
authentic enough to express it

and not give in to the urge to remake it
in its own image, to say

what that sprig of sage meant
and what it had become, rather than

what it was. This isn't
an argument about Zen

or any other contraption for incarcerating
the things of the world in meaning.

Memory knows what it wants,
and what it wants is not the past.

Pound may have had it right. Maybe
meaning *is* a matter of adding on

stroke after stroke until what's on the page
houses enough fragments to form

something whole. That sprig of sage
shrouded with the haunt of its scent.

The Carcass of What Was

An ambulance shreds whatever silence
might've been a threat tonight, carrying
the frail, bitter remnant of an old god
who sucks in oxygen like it could be
the last descendant of nectar. No prayer
will mean, tonight, anything more or less
than it would any other night. A mask
making it giddy with air, this carcass
of what once was worshipped isn't in need
of anything as mundane as language.

Leaving a Place of Smoke and Dire Prophesies

This sky seems too sure to argue with. Storms
have a way of getting things done. Even
the woman no one in town wants to remember
the name of, who whispers stories of sharks
and warm drinks made of coconut and leaves
the bar, grinning, with storms, would have to admit
this much is true. The mystery of storms
has to do with where it is they start off.

To believe one place can have any edge
over another is to fall victim to
the oldest scam around. Origin
has nothing to say about us that's any kind of
answer. Any sky we can cozy up to has to be
worth the effort. Women at the other end
of the bar laugh and their hands flutter
signs into the smoke couples dance through

to the lazy blues riffs someone's paid for
with a stack of quarters, ephemeral signs
that warn of storms coming that won't
forgive even the most innocent. Judgment
isn't anything any one of us can ever be
prepared for. Step out of this place of smoke
and blues and dire prophesies, grinning
like a shark, knowing this argument's yours.

Despite Heraclitus

If I'm nothing but the argument I have
every day with the sky, make it a good one.

The sky, not the argument. A crow, contentious
in flight, stitches the barren branches

of maples and oaks to the more obvious
constant flux of cirrus and cumulus. Heraclitus

said all of it's changing. What we label the past
isn't any more stable than the evidence

I rely on as proof that a woman's savage beauty
doesn't have to tear apart whatever memory

huddles in a cardboard box leaned up against
the bitter, graffitied curve of my heart. The past

is always full of homeless, and what they ask for
isn't what you'd think. *Don't deny us*

our passion, they plead. *Without that,*
every rough alphabet scrawled on these overpasses

remains nonsense, they say. The sky doesn't
take sides. When it comes to passion, it has

nothing to say. Any argument about love
has to be the opposite of aerodynamic in design.

When the storm comes, and it will come, love
itself has to hunker down and lean into it

with all its weight. Let the sky and all
its named and anonymous formations of vapor

amaze us from enough of a distance to leave
room for rough letters—scrawled on cement arches

under bridges that hum sonatas of departure—
to coalesce into a sentence that, misread

from the distance a crow flies, completes an ode
to a woman constant enough to love.

The Weatherman Breaks Down and
Comes Clean a Little After 3 a.m.

Forecasting's not what we do. Nor do we
control anything. No more than dancers
who claim rain follows them and falls because
of the message their feet pound into dirt.
It's just I love how air's more substantial
after the kind of rain said to soak streets.
Which of course it can't. So much of what's said
doesn't come close to touching what it's said
to mean. Even this, most of you asleep,
me confessing all we do here is watch.

To Die in Erie, Pennsylvania

after Richard Hugo

Accept water knows which direction's true
north. That the lake knows what it means
to have to fold or lose it all. That snow
echoes the persistent chants of the ghosts
of women who believe their men, gone
hunting, will hear their voices and turn back
for love. Local TV stations call each other out
on innocuous details. Loss is behind

all programming, though no one knows whose loss
it is. Rumors of ancient eels or sea mollusks
gone so very wrong far below the lake's surface
keep most folks from diving in for a swim.
One sad drunk spends his fetid summer nights
strumming a guitar and singing songs of love
to the hidden monsters of the lake. Women
bring him food to keep up his strength, and men
drink with him between songs, telling stories
of sightings. Later at home and in bed

with the women, they speculate which rumor
has it right. It's some Iroquois ghost lost
and bitter, the drunk says, no one there
to hear. How he loses at solitaire for hours
on end is enough to break the heart of
any monster, ghost or not. To die in Erie,
do it when the ice is thick enough to let you
dance north to Canada to the howls of a ghost.

A Few Lines Stolen from Keats

Look, a boy, ten, tells his sister, pointing
to a sky as much an anomaly
as anything's ever been. *It has*

forgotten us. To say anything's writ
in the night sky in the pathetic
flickerings of dead and dying light

requires faith in the undefined always
left at the end of saying. We will
always be forgotten. And the night sky

never had a single word to say
about the envy a boy feels
when his sister's remembering

being kissed the night before
in the backseat of a Ford pickup
by a boy old enough to think

he deserves everything a few lines
stolen from Keats
can get him. Nostalgia

is what we say gets us past
the stuttering awkwardness
of the way things really happened.

It's a kind of forgiveness, or pity.
Or maybe a soothing balm.
The boy's sister will forget how her lips

uttered sounds she hadn't
known she could make
and words she knew she wasn't

supposed to say. How she let
her little brother change
everything with some innocent comment

on the winter constellations. How
those dimmer stars can't
hold on to anything, not even

the shapes they were given so long ago
by men who believed
the stars took up the stories

we need to be reminded of. Notes,
a kind of celestial shorthand,
was what they became. Stories,

she's learned, are what men do
to all of it, the world
they just can't leave be. And nothing

men make of the world, no matter
how pretty the words
they say it in, will ever be as sacred

as the world was before they made it
into something. The girl believes
this, and hugs her little brother under a sky

she knows isn't what he wants
it to be. Amnesia, after
all, she believes, is a blessing.

A Temporary Delaying of the Inevitable

in memory of Deborah Digges

So much of memory has someone dressed
for forgiveness, or forgiving. The light

comes from somewhere behind at an angle
that could mean it's meant to deceive,

and if there's music playing off in the distance
it's either something Mozart would've penned

or the sort of jazz that's so watered down
it's anonymous. To be sure, music

longs to live in the body without need
of nomenclature, to busy itself

with the past as if it were preparing for
a party where every guest is masked

and refuses to offer any clue
who they really are. Guessing is more fun

than knowing, they say, and Auden nods
in his corner, behind his garish mask

meant to resemble the splendid visage
of whatever water bird is local.

Maybe the blue heron, its slender neck
curled up in imitation of a sage

question mark. So much for masks,
a woman whispers who recognizes bitterness

when she sees it on the face of a ghost.
Even the most elaborate disguise

doesn't get past her without first being
seen through, down to the bone. Auden's

lack of something under the skin
gives him away, she says. It reminds her

how easy it is to forgive the dead
whatever faults they cling to. Memory

is an elaborate mask the dead have
to wear, if they want to be remembered,

and either forgives too much or condemns
the dead, she says, in ways that deny them

the chance to argue who they really were.
Living is more jolly than not being

around, the ghost of a bitter poet
might like to say, if he still had a mouth

and the tongue to make the transcendent noise
words are. The masked ball we're invited to,

both the living and the dead, is lit up
by what seem to be carnival klieg lights,

the kind that would be pointed up to catch
the trapeze artist, dressed in gleaming tights

that forgive nothing, even way up there,
far enough off even a measly dime,

held in front of an eye behind a mask,
would block the entire, brilliant body

lit up by the klieg light in that moment
just before the legs push off and it flies

toward a swing let go of at the same time
as a means of salvation. The music

that fills the tent, as the body hurtles
toward death or a temporary delay

of the inevitable, is almost
grotesque in its cheeriness. It could be

a kind of hope in quarter-time, maybe
a whistling in the dark, or a tune

the trapeze artist loves and wouldn't mind
being the last thing he would hear

in this accidental world. The mask
he wears hurtling through air is the visage

of the austere poet whose poem about
Icarus forgives the ploughman, the sun,

and the delicate ship sailing calmly away
from the pale and shivering legs

of the haughty boy whose father's sorrow
has become the sky. The trapeze artist

would not be out of place if he walked in to
the party. Grounded, though, would he want

to stick around? If he saw, across the room,
an earnest, middle-aged woman who looks

as if she knows ghosts, wearing, as a mask,
the face of a house sparrow with the look

of some evening prayer, he'd want to stay
long enough to make his way over to

where she's holding court. The trapeze artist
would want to hear her tell of his tumbling

through air, believing that in her telling of it
he would find, finally, the memory

of flying through the air he had always
wanted. Listening to his sore body

in the conviction of her voice, he's sure,
would let him, finally, forgive the air.

After the Carnival Closes Down

Gravity, at times, goes slack, like the night
the Ferris wheel lifted a woman to the moon.
Believe you could go back and find the carnival
with its canned, pitiful version of exotic music
and let the Ferris wheel lift you into a future
you imagined with your back flat on the earth
night after night. The absence the Ferris wheel

stands in for, with its gaudy lights visible for miles,
is enough to scare you on to rides more linear
and closer to the ground, where gravity is
less of a concern. Despite bulbs where suckers
would be, the black tentacles of the Octopus,
spinning and looping and dipping, stay close enough
to the horizon you can breathe without gasping.

Sorrow, though, makes of the heart a carnie game,
rigged, where the prizes collapse into dust
on the haphazard shelves, winning not an option.
What happened to the woman who touched the moon
isn't a story gravity's concerned with,
and laughter has a history of absence and recurrence.
The moon prefers being low to the horizon,
close enough you could tie a string to it and take it home.

Swear Not by the Moon, th' Inconstant Moon

—William Shakespeare

I was ten when the moon stopped being
the moon, all that kicking up dust eons old
seemed so irreverent. Though I didn't know

that word, I knew respect was due. More
than those ghostly, herky-jerky figures leaping,
danseurs in a low-budget ballet, could offer.

Now the moon's just reflected light, the dull
story of abandoned equipment, and a flag,

American, built to give the illusion
of a wind not there, a fluttering purely show.

Maybe to know it's there is enough. As a boy,
though, to lose the moon was more
disturbing than any gains I could imagine.

Not knowing the moon had let us
believe we were watched over. Too much
knowing has left us older, on our own.

Last Words to My Father

It's terrible, Father, to imagine
the loneliness, those last days and nights
in that place with so many
rooms filled with waiting, you
only one form the waiting

took. In formless gowns open
in the back, waiting
shuffled the corridors and lay in dim rooms
bathed with the banal
flickering of TVs, bad reception

not worth a curse. Better
to believe that wasn't you
jerking your legs, shriveled enough
under thin hospital sheets
walking wasn't a question. Not you,

staring, most of my final visit,
at a bare wall, the flickers of faint shadows
all you could recognize. Nothing
left but to forgive the inarticulate curses
your knuckles wrote on my back

all those years ago, anger and alcohol
the way you translated, then,
everything foreign to you. Terrible,
Father, is a word fists know,
and the consolation of forgiveness isn't

a cure for dementia. I can't help
but wonder what you would
have to say to this. One thing
I'm sure of, Father. You
would've loved the petite woman

the honor guard included,
her face so pale and determined
you might have mistaken her
for an angel. You would have
stood next to her while another soldier

played a rendition of "Taps"
so—forgive me, Father—heartfelt
I thought of Orpheus
and his music after he lost his wife
the second time. You were being

placed in the ground next to
your first wife, my mother.
Your second shivered at the plaintive horn
in the damp February morning. Go on,
Father. Flirt with the woman

no uniform can disguise. Make her
laugh and feel—no longer
an angel, just another waitress or
salesgirl or stranger on a bus—anything
is possible. Make her believe being

alive isn't as terrible as it feels
when we love the dead
and have to forgive ourselves, the way
I have to forgive myself how I forgive you,
Father, dead and still flirting.

The Head, in Profile, of an Ibis

If our dead watch us, do they
turn away when we do
something they don't

approve of? Do the dead
remember what it is to be

embarrassed? Mother, do you
say you don't know me

when the other dead ask?
Are you ashamed you have to
forgive me for doing things

your church named sins? All you knew,
alive, was disappointment

in what they said should bring you
joy. It's all about being

good, they said. Was it
worth it, Mother, having two sons
with a man who drank too much

and couldn't forgive himself
some trespass he could never admit?

Did he, finally, love you, his
touch a hieroglyph you knew enough

not to decipher? The animals
in us, stiff and horizontal,
house the most profound expressions

of what we like to say
is our better nature. Love

has the head, in profile, of an ibis,
and sings hymns the dead know

by heart. Do you, Mother, still
try to sing me to sleep?

Surely the dead don't still feel
the need to care for us.

An ibis calls out this morning,
its song something
both the dead and the living love.

Early Pastoral

for Diane

Morning glares, crisp, on a lawn freshly-mown.
In the shadow of a bird feeder, sparrows

ask of the shorn grass nothing but the fallen
bird seed, and in this light everything is

granted. Not even the dulled absence of
meaning could ruin this moment. A finch

flashes its cartoon yellow from one edge
of a stunted tree's shadow and explodes

in this light that, if it had a voice, would
no doubt whisper *golden* as it revels

in leaping from that bedlam of feathers
and insistence in a way that seems to,

just now, scar this landscape with a fever
of color. A cardinal in the shade,

a male, despite its being distinguished
for its brilliance, has no time this morning

for something as shrill as jealousy. This
morning's business is the sharing of light,

and, no matter how much any bird claims,
no abundance of color ruins this world.

Before All Hell Breaks Loose

Exhausted, it's not too dense—the chaos
of morning grackle chatter. All language
is a question of perspective, meaning,
at times, too much to ask for. Nothing less
than a rude babel of bird song torches
the shrubs, igniting another last day
before all hell breaks loose. I've heard it said
we're living in the end times. Try telling
the grackles the weary world's winding down.
Music's a language that says time won't end.

Stories of Blue Herons in Late Winter

The somber itch of crows in a gray sky
in March. A slant of light twitches

and carves the landscape, stark
sparrows punctuating whatever sad,

languid sentences might have been said
with no one listening. This cold morning

even the sparrows seem condescending
under a sky so indifferent. A woman

runs alongside a boy no more than ten.
The kite the boy's trying to keep aloft

is fashioned in the iconic shape of a blue heron,
a bird the boy's never seen. He thinks

the kite is the shape of a myth. Let it be
years before he knows how wrong he is.

This bird-kite slants toward the ground,
twitching in an inconstant wind. When it lifts

toward a sky gray enough to bring a man
to tears, the woman laughs and urges her son

to keep on running. *Don't stop,* she yells,
and he runs, the kite a hieroglyph come to life.

The Rough Grace of Syllabics

Pain comes from the darkness
And we call it wisdom. It is pain.
—Randall Jarrell

Desolation makes hoarders even of saints,
their shelves lined with parts vaguely bird.
Any less sorrow and I might be able to
speak in syllabics and charm my way through.
More images, a woman once whispered.
Take her face I tried to sketch and ruined
with inadequate lines. A mask is
all it is. Lifeless. Nowhere near to her
exquisite grace, which defies definition. Still,
such a mask, covered with the rough scrawls of
what could be a language primitive enough
to speak of love to saints, might provide solace.

Almost a Sonnet on a Train to Points West

for Rachelle

Outside, a rendition of stubborn weather
that doesn't know when to give up.
Just enough light to imagine Toledo, Ohio
as it goes by. This could all be evidence
no woman could refute, or just proof of
the inarticulate nature of longing. Even this
dour landscape, shrouded and being forgotten,
is enough to convince me loneliness has
an agenda. All the women on this train
shrouded in black dresses that only hint
at bodies, speaking a foreign tongue,
become the prayer they've always been.
A prayer even weather must bow down to
and an irreverent woman all but refutes.

With Walt Whitman in a Couple of Hotel Rooms

A girl claps, timing her dance through the lobby
of this hotel full of girls so young and excited
to be somewhere other than home they could be
mistaken for being drunk, the way their laughter

knocks them off balance when the elevator doors open.
They are cheerleaders, it turns out, gathered
for a regional contest. These girls, whose job it is
to draw crowds into some game are, themselves,

to *be* the game. To be *both in and out of the game,*
Whitman wrote more than a hundred years ago.
I wonder what words he would have used to touch
the young, athletic girls giggling these narrow halls.

Once, I tried to memorize the body of a woman
asleep in morning light in a hotel bed, wanting
to experience her form in those tangled sheets
more fully than I had ever experienced any presence,

or absence. When she stretched, revealing
the elucidation of hip bone shadows, my tongue
wanted to articulate that angular pressing of
what lies beneath the flesh out against the flesh.

Longing reminds us how little words can contain,
or conjure. Not even the distance that kept me

from lying with her in that bed when, still half-
asleep and half-clad and half-drunk, she invited me.

Not even how I curse myself for not accepting
that invitation. Just to have lain beside her.
Whatever you lost, Walt, it doesn't come close.
Not even these half-nude, giggling bodies dancing

the dimly-lit halls of this gaudy hotel tonight can ease
the longing I'm cursed to acknowledge. Love is
as often expressed in not having as in having, and memory
longs for what we didn't do as often as the done.

A Decade Ago in a Hospital in Pittsburgh

It's not so much the naked body of this
sixteen-year-old girl forsaken beneath a sheet

of what looks to be cloth but is, in fact,
only paper. And it's not that this is

only memory and the memory of the girl,
or the woman she will become, and not

mine. It's that memory isn't history, but more
a shadow screen on which our hands

take what shapes they can and try to reshape,
with the light and a limited vocabulary,

what happened so what happened better fits
our fictions and desires. Like this longing I have

to walk into that psych ward and get under
the stiff paper with that naked girl and hold her

and whisper a future to her that includes me
holding her, to unlock the shackles on her wrists

and ankles and kiss the chafe marks. A poet
once argued that tenderness is a word only

those who have experienced the absence of it
can say. I don't want this naked girl to ever be

able to say the word, but no doubt she will.
I cannot assure its presence, and no rough shape

formed by the shadow of anyone's hands can
form the hieroglyphs that would spell out longing,

or touch this naked girl or the woman
she will become so she can forgive herself.

The Singing of Accidental Larks

Absinthe, a woman said, cures memory.

In the gymnasium her body danced in,
mats retain the pressure of her delicate hands,

proof of a divinity in the flesh
of a body too full of grace to topple

into anything close to ruin. Believing
absence could be any kind of answer

is a lark, and a lark is a bird
whose song can often make us forget

time ignores us. When I imagine
her innate grace as she tumbled

with precision in time to a music
no instrument readily forms,

the crowd is yelling at me to go on
and slip into any sacramental amnesia

that will have me. Listening to the lark
that must have flown in by accident

and gotten trapped in this empty space
lit by the warm glow of polished wood

might be a way out. Or maybe
absinthe *is* the only cure. To love

has often been said to involve falling,
so these tumblers' mats belong,

though a gymnasium's not even close
to a fitting home for the indefensible

dismounts the heart keeps trying to nail.
The heart's not adept at tumbling,

or balancing on the parallel bars.
To dance, without caring

what anyone might think,
along those slender laths of teak

or oak polished enough to enfold
the dancer in a light that could turn

a woman into nothing that could lead to
any sorrow might be enough

to make the heart have faith its legs are
the firm, agile legs of a gymnast,

and believe the song of a lark's pure absinthe.

The Hip Bones of a Woman as Runes

Even a god can thirst
for words
—Douglas Smith

It's subverbal, see, how the hip bones
of an elegant young woman elucidate

the precise mechanism behind what is said
to be memory. Runes in flesh,

so archaic as to be meaningless, still
don't cross over into nonsense. Dances

the body dances asleep are half-longed-for
or half-forgotten. Desire

comes with a degree of difficulty
that leads to the false inflation of its scores,

less a competition than an exhibition
of what isn't true. A knit sweater frames

a concave belly edged by runes that signify
the carrying of another is possible,

and this makes for an elegy only longing
can translate with any accuracy. *Datta.* What's given

isn't given with any expectation other
than the giving, and without the possibility

of loss, of absence, the body hesitates
and is lost indeed. *Dayadhvam.* Love is,

after all, a longing for the other. The body needs
the erudition of touch and the fictions

that accompany touch in the remembering of it.
Damyata. The abstract handcuffs the body

to time, which is always planning to escape, taking
the shackled flesh with it out of necessity.

Memory must reconcile what is left behind
in the prison break. Those hip bones

and the not-touching of them, and all the longing
the not-touching disguises, is the best argument

to be made for positing meaning, no matter
how tenuous it may be, in the body Blake wanted

to sing the experience of in the most innocent
of psalms. Even the terror that is the first

touch of beauty sings the history of the coming
together of bone and flesh. To chant,

as if in desperate homage, the shadowy runes
formed by the hip bones of a particular woman

at a particular moment of sleep and loss
is a futile gesture of remembering,

a desolate doff of a cap to the unending longing
that is the mute companion of the not-done.

What Stone's on Hand

Starlings trill baroque concertos in the trees
in the moon-scythed dark. Statues stroke

the long, stone faces of horses they offer sugar
before heading off to bars for bourbons

with beer chasers. They feed the jukebox
to hear songs the bartender's forgotten

the lyrics to but not the tunes. Nostalgia
carves us out of whatever stone's on hand.

Pony up the coins to challenge the statue
of some drunk civil war general to pool.

Don't let him distract you with lines he stole
from Whitman he wants you to think are his.

He plays every angle with a placid intimacy
he comes by honestly. All those harsh edges.

The moon, though, has to pull off bank shots
no one would be fool enough to bet on

just to be allowed to stay in the sky
long and full enough to be remembered.

Statues are not immune to being
infected by memory just because they are

made of granite or stone that pretends to be
marble. The way those starlings, trilling,

pretend to chamber music. The night has
room enough and music for all that's past.

To Account for Such Grace

Some nights, light's particle nature is italicized
by the downward emphasis of a steady rain.

A woman without an umbrella's a frail shadow
hunched over a flame flickering between

her palms in a shallow alcove, the only light
the flame in her hands and a sixty-watt bulb

somewhere behind her in the niche she's found
that almost keeps her out of the frenzied rain.

If this were being painted in 16th century Florence,
the woman would be the only woman

the church could love, the mother of God
the son, and cupped in her delicate, trembling hands

would be the burning heart of God become man,
having flown out his dying chest with a last wheeze

from the cross. Rain, in the painting, would be
an occasion for the artist to show off his brilliance

with reflective surfaces, nothing more. History
would have us ignore how the woman's hands

tremble and seem too delicate to hold up
under her grief. No matter is as delicate

as light. Or as alluring as the face of this woman,
having a smoke, waiting out the rain. Entire

histories have been imagined to account for
such grace. Music transforms the human voice

to make possible even a vague hint of the delicacy
of this woman's fragrant hands, moist with mist,

reflecting light in ways a Renaissance master
would have bowed down to, envious, rapt.

On the Eaves of the House Next Door

The music of sparrows arguing turns at the feeder
is enough to get this hunkering ghost

who had forgotten the world had music in it
to hum some tune Sinatra made his own.

Set to motion by the subtle almost-music
rising out of what used to be his throat, the ghost

dances a waltz elaborate enough to make him grin.
How much can the presence of a grinning ghost mean

to the fragrant woman refilling the feeder and singing
to the sparrows perched on neighboring trees

or the eaves of the house next door, expectant
and nervous? The ghost is taken with the woman

and wants to ask her to join him and Sinatra in the dance.
The light's angled just enough for her to convince herself

the insubstantial figure of a man is stuttering beside her,
holding out his hand as if to offer to swing her

into some aberrant waltz the music of sparrows
makes possible. If she takes the ghost's hand,

would any one of us driving by on our way home
be cruel enough, or broken enough, to deny her

the pleasure of such a waltz on a day
the light is skewed enough we might see

a dead lover grinning in the passenger seat
and believe if we just keep on driving

we'll find a place to pull off and park
and make love with the one who has always

been there in the midst of any passion?
Let this woman waltz with the sparrows.

Let that waltz make everything possible.

Early Light in Erie

Morning, reflected, assumes these buildings the way gulls
assume the ambivalent sky at the edge of the bay

blocks north. The chatter of gulls here is less cacophony
and more a lonesome blues riff strummed lazily on

an acoustic guitar salvaged from a dusty second-hand shop
for less than ten bucks. All that's constructed dissolves

in this light. All movement's a huddling together,
an embrace, romantic. A woman throws stale bread

to gulls and the rock doves we call pigeons, and the birds
ignore each other in the rush and stuttering of wings.

Give us this day our daily bread, this woman says, having
chosen kindness. I'd like to say this early light has

chosen to illuminate these buildings. That every music,
whether composed or the result of a moment's collusion

of disparate sounds, is an urgent declaration of compassion,
instinctual or not. The bay I could walk to in minutes

should be more than enough to cleanse what we say
is inside us—the soul. Reflected off the vastness

of windows meant to reveal what's inside, this light
seems to burn enough to consume the world in fire.

This has to be enough to purify the soul, and to join everything in this moment in a gesture that blesses it all.